**Praise and Reviews for**

A Manager's Guide To
## MAXIMIZING SEARCH FIRM
# SUCCESS

"Frank Risalvato has hit a home run with his book: 'Maximizing Search Firm Success.' There is no fluff, only sound reasoning and guidance rooted in real world experience offering help so hiring managers make the right decision every time. 'Maximizing Search Firm Success' should be on the desk of every hiring authority as a reference."

—**David A. Knutson, CPC, President** The Knutson Group, LLC
*Hall of Fame 2005 Inductee - National Association of Personnel Services*
*Co-Founder, International Retained Search Association (IRSA)*
*Past President of the Board, Arizona Staffing Professionals Association*

"Frank Risalvato's 'Maximizing Search Firm Success' should be purchased by the pallet-load by every search firm owner for distributing to their clients. By heightening your client's awareness of the behind-the-scenes differences in recruiting formats, this book will surely boost every recruiting firm's productivity while eliminating unnecessary repetition and enhancing client company's results."

—**Orrick G. Nepomuceno, CPC**
**Author of** *Hitchhiker In The Corner Office*

*"As an executive and attorney who has been on both sides of the recruiting process — hiring others as well as being hired myself — 'Maximizing Search Firm Success' has alerted my awareness on the advantages of developing a high quality partnership with one single executive recruiter versus a shallow relationship with a multitude of recruiters. It is an absolute must read before signing any search firm agreement."*

**—Michael Belinski, Esq. CPCU**
Critical Path Management Consultants LLC, Washington, D.C.


*"The advice in Frank's 'Maximizing Search Firm Success' book would have spared a recent client I know a lot of pain and convincing. It also provides insight into why many corporate HR recruiting practices are counter productive and how a strong recruiting organization will actually save both time and money in the long run. Frank makes very compelling arguments to these points."*

**—Andrew Buck, PMP Managing Partner**, General National
Consulting of New York and London
www.generalnational.com


*"Frank Risalvato's book is a must read for anyone who is a company owner, manager, or executive that is impacted by today's ever-changing human resources and recruiting dynamics. He presents, in an easy, straight forward, no holds barred fashion, effective solutions to problems that companies and search firms alike deal with every day. Every office manager should have a copy for both reference and training everyone involved with hiring."*

**—Scott LeCompte, Sr. Vice President / Principal**, Blackburn
Group Inc. / MSA RiskPro.com

"Finally, we have a play book that line managers, human resource professionals and those involved in talent acquisition can use to help their teams win the war for the best and brightest talent. Frank demystifies the use of search professionals (aka headhunters) and provides valuable insight into selecting and working with recruiting firms. The book provides an easy to understand blueprint for creating and implementing mutual accountabilities and expectations between any organization and a prospective or existing staffing partner."

—**Jeff Kaye, CEO** of Kaye/Bassman International and
Next Level Recruiting Training
Largest single site search firm in the country


"Highly recommend this for anyone who has the responsibility to hire, as well as those of us in the search field who should be sharing this guide with our hiring clientele for educational purposes!"

—**Brian Stutt, CPC, CEO**, The MedPoint Group

*A Manager's Guide To*

# MAXIMIZING SEARCH FIRM
# SUCCESS

## TURNING PRE-CONCEIVED NOTIONS OF RECRUITING FIRMS ON THEIR HEAD

*Includes the*
**Top 10**
*Causes of Client/Search Firm Breakdown*

Frank G. Risalvato, CPC

**A Manager's Guide To Maximizing Search Firm Success**

© 2010 by Frank G. Risalvato, CPC

All Rights Reserved

Searchlight Publishing
P.O. Box 77927
Charlotte, N.C. 28271
(704) 243-2110

This publication is designed to provide accurate and authoritative information regarding the subject matter herein. It is sold with the understanding that the publisher is not engaged in legal, accounting, or other professional services. If legal advice is required, or other expert assistance is required, the services of a competent professional should be sought.

ISBN# 978-0-9830593-0-1

Cover & Interior Design by
Scribe Freelance Book Design Company

*Printed in the United States of America*

*This book is dedicated to Deborah, Frank Junior, and Rebecca.*

*Without their patience, tolerance and contagious, cheerful encouragement
I would not be as complete an individual as I am.*

# TABLE OF CONTENTS

Acknowledgments                                                    XI

Preface                                                          XIII

Foreword                                                          XV

Introduction                                                    XVII

Chapter 1: Origins of Client Company/Search Firm Breakdown        21

Chapter 2: Top Ten Causes of Client/Search Firm Breakdown         25

Chapter 3: More Solutions for Search Firm Success                 49

Chapter 4: A Brief History of Fee-Based Recruiting                51

Chapter 5: Contingency Versus Retained Agreements                 55

Chapter 6: How to Choose a Search Firm                            73

Chapter 7: Summary and Conclusion                                 81

Appendix                                                          87

Works Cited                                                       91

About the Author                                                  93

Notes                                                             95

# ACKNOWLEDGMENTS

I wish to thank my editor Mark Boone of Chicago who exhibited saintly patience while I threw all sorts of temper tantrums at his red-lining and axing entire segments of what I thought was my best material. He was right and without him this would look more like a collective jumble of notes.

Thanks to my wife Debbie who tolerates my tirades and crazy ideas and for actually believing we'd get to the finish line. I often wonder why she puts up with me. Thanks to Paul Hawkinson, my surrogate father-of-sorts, (or brother-in-law) for telling me what a "good little writer you are kid" and instilling the confidence I needed to finish this project.

I must also extend gratitude for tremendous help contributed by other giants of the search and recruiting industry such as Andrew Buck of General National, LLC in New York and Bob Corlett of Staffing Advisors of Washington D.C. In between speeding across the Atlantic in jets and leaping into elevators on his way up to the office suites of skyscrapers, Andrew was always prompt in getting back to me and Bob Corlett has a way with words like few others.

My appreciation and gratefulness is also extended to Douglas Beabout, CPC, whom I've bumped into at national recruiting conventions and conferences in several cities over the years and developed a kinship of sorts. Doug is one of those guys that can transform an average event into a classy one just by walking into the room. He holds dear some of the highest levels of integrity I have ever encountered in a fiercely competitive industry where such qualities can be challenging to find.

I must also thank the real estate agents and other professionals I consulted with to make sure we were as factual as possible when making industry comparisons. Special thanks are also in order for all the recruiting firm owners, managers, and company presidents all over the country I continuously emailed, pestered and called to corroborate, compare and validate the subject matter covered.

Thanks to the various national, regional, and state recruiting associations that invited me to speak on the subject of client education all over the U.S. For a while I had a semi-full time job of hop-scotching from one resort to another to discuss the subject of client outreach in our seminars. As much fun as those conventions are returning to my humble home and wife was a welcome reprieve.

I'm grateful to God for the blessed life I've had and for having the health, vigor and energy to see this project finalized into the current form.

# PREFACE

The origins of this manual started more than a decade ago when a fifteen-page guide we had created for internal use at Inter-Regional Executive Search was discovered to be helpful by clients that never had any other search or recruiting firm provide them with such an instructional primer. Most only knew what was handed down from generations of former managers, and unfortunately much of that information passed along was either distorted or obsolete.

Back then the guide was designed for a quick and simple read. We took notice that hiring managers were actually following our tips and suggestions resulting in measurable increases in staffing productivity. As word spread through trade and professional association events which I often am asked to participate in, it eventually piqued the interest of the editor of a search industry monthly publication. We offered a condensed, specially-modified, excerpted version to *The Fordyce Letter©*, which was considered for decades to be the premium monthly newsletter for both retained and contingency-based recruiters.

To my surprise then-editor Paul Hawkinson featured elements of our instructional manual not only within the publication, but as the feature front cover story of the December 2006 edition. This further fueled what eventually became global interest which continued for months and years afterwards. Emails and calls arrived from as far as Singapore, Luxemborg, South Africa, New Zealand, Australia, and all over North America requesting examples and information about how we were using our "Maximizing Search Firm Success" outreach guide. The spike of visitors to our searchwizardry.com adjunct training site was evidence that the recruiting industry craved and deserved something more.

The problem was our original guide was written and intended for IRES clients only. To create something which appealed to a wider audience and useful to both recruiters, human resources, and executive management required cracking our knuckles and going back to the drawing board. So I embarked on my next voyage to expand and improve upon our original version so that readers from all walks of life, including corporate talent acquisition and management professionals, could better appreciate and understand the dynamics and intricacies of recruiting in a way never before explained.

I stopped counting sometime after the eighth edit as to how many re-writes this project required. The stress and strain of the never-ending and tedious editing process that went on for years took its toll on my children, wife and quite possibly on my regal beagle, Lucy who impatiently hopped and danced by the door for what must have been hours to finally get her needed walk outside. I spent many nights working until the wee-hours — since that was the only quiet time I could carve out in my day — and was too happy to return to a normal sleep schedule and recuperate when this was finally submitted to press.

It is my hope that search firm owners of national franchises, multi-site and single-site offices all find this worthy of stocking up on and handing out to clients as a great educational supplement that will reap dividends through mutual appreciation of one-another's services.

For everyone else who picks up a copy or had one recommended, I hope you are left with a more informed introspect into an admittedly nebulous industry that has many facets.

# FOREWORD

You are either always growing, or otherwise dying.

This quotation has been made by many management executives of corporations and even professional sport franchises.

The single most critical element in an employer's success and growth is attracting those talented people who are essential to the organization's ability to meet such goals. An employer's economic stability and recovery are dramatically affected by how effectively they adopt the best practices of talent acquisition. At times though, the most well-intentioned recruiting programs and processes stop short of finding the best talent available.

When an employer and a professional recruiter enter into a relationship focused on finding and hiring that uniquely talented professional the outcome should be successful on the first go-around. It should not require extra innings or overtime play. Yet professional recruiters and employers often find themselves as opponents or adversaries.

For the first time in my career as a professional recruiter and national search firm trainer, which extends back several decades, we have the missing piece that may unite both parties and eliminate resistance to the best practices available. A strategically solid, time-tested resource that empowers employers to avail themselves of the highest levels of skill, service, professionalism and results they seek from the executive recruiter or staffing professional they choose. This competitive employer advantage is the book you hold.

Talent acquisition is facing the most competitive era in history. While there is a blizzard of electronic information available on every website, managing the mushrooming resources ahead of your competition requires a dedicated professional more than ever.

Every company hiring manager, from the warehouse logistics supervisor to the chief financial officer, requires trusted advisors. Now you know, once and for all, how to best utilize a search firm and recruiter. Frank Risalvato has crafted this powerful and competitive resource within the crucible of his own successful executive recruiting career.

In my three decades of experience as a practicing search consultant, industry speaker and international trainer, I have had the opportunity to meet many of the best in the recruiting industry. I place Frank high on that very small list. Frank brings that rare and powerful combination of skills, wisdom, and experience to bear for many employers whose success and growth are ensured by the constant and consistent ability to recruit the highest caliber talent.

I am proud to know Frank Risalvato and know our industry has benefitted from his contributions. I know you will come to know him as well when you read this wonderful and timeless work, *A Hiring Manager's Guide To Maximizing Search Firm Success.*

**—Doug Beabout, CPC, CSP**
The Douglas Howard Group
*International search industry trainer and lecturer*

# INTRODUCTION

Perhaps you have wondered how a search firm which came recommended by management ever made it on to the company "preferred vendor list". And if the search firm you are considering to use is not on the corporate vendor list, how does a mid or upper level manager get such a firm approved?

What are the best contract terms? Should you consider contingency, retained, or some combination thereof when it comes to compensation structure? All these questions and more will be answered by this book.

Once you have found a reputable search firm with which you're about to settle into a recruiting agreement, you must consider "What next?" For starters we must understand that in order for the partnership to succeed a symbiotic relationship must occur between the client company and the search firm's recruiting representative.

Contracting an executive recruiter is not unlike hiring an expert fishing guide who knows where certain type of trophy bass congregate, what lures, bait and tackle should be used depending on time of day and season of the year — and the exact rate of speed to cast your line and reel it in so as to not spook the fish. The primary difference being that a fishing or hunting guide will most likely want payment upfront in exchange for his services before he reveals his secrets and spends an entire day or weekend pointing out prime locations.

The guide's wealth of knowledge comes from years of practice and learning combined with continuous study. Moon phases, barometric pressure, weather patterns, seasonal bait cycles are just a few of the considerations which make up the guide's art and science.

As with any business transaction, you get what you pay for. The guide's services may not be inexpensive, but your use of such may increase the odds of getting a picture taken with a prized catch worthy of boasting about as well as maximizing the results, given your limited time available for such outdoor recreation.

The recruiting firm relationship is no different. After all, one of the end results most decision-makers get to see is little more than a resume with a cover note leading one to justifiably think: *"Is it really little more than making phone calls, sending e-mails, and initiating dialogue with prospective candidates?"*

Yes. It involves more. Much more.

While a search firm can assist in significantly increasing the percentage of premium talent identified — just as our fishing guide would increase the likelihood of hooking more trophy bass — it inevitably becomes the company hiring authority's responsibility for reacting correctly when reeling such talent in and ensuring that it does not flop out of the boat.

Much of the criticism and unfair rumors about recruiting firms generally stem from a breakdown in this "handing off" process. The hand-off is a specific point where the executive search professional hands the process off to the hiring manager. While the executive search consultant may be dealing with multiple interviews weekly, and may be negotiating hires semi-weekly (this varies according to hierarchy levels) the full-time business manager is primarily responsible for his or her department and may get involved in only a few hires each year to support her primary role.

There are other reasons search firms may fail to produce from a client company's perspective. The most common reasons for failure are outlined in Chapter 2 of this manual. They have been distilled from hundreds of millions of dollars of assignments over a twenty-year period.

Great effort has been expended to include information uncovered not only by IRES associates but also reaffirmed and validated via the training of hundreds of recruiting professionals at peer search firms and from leading industry training seminars and webinars for national and international trade associations.

Chapter 5 discusses the three main compensation arrangements: Retained, Contingency, and Hybrid Search. It outlines the advantages and drawbacks of each. Chapter 6 offers ideas on how to go about choosing and selecting a search firm.

There are many search firms and recruiters which, to be sure, ought not to be in existence. And indeed, the market and economy eventually flush them out. Some are amateurish in approach. Others never achieve a level beyond mediocrity in a limited geographic area. This is an unfortunate result of an industry that is autonomously operated at the local level and as diverse as the hundreds of industries and thousands of functional disciplines it specializes in.

In the majority of our studies, breakdowns between the hiring company and the search firm often involved companies requesting assistance after protracted recruiting periods that led to no hirable candidate. Many of the issues we identified usually occurred during the transition period when the recruiter handed off the candidate to a client manager. Similar to when the fishing guide hands the fishing rod over to the weekend angler during the reeling-in process.

Angling is however, much more simplistic as the fish are for the most part genetically programmed to react to bait while candidates require a far more sophisticated approach, specialized industry knowledge, as well as cultivation of trust and a degree of mutual respect and understanding.

This guide will help you identify the most common problems that can arise so that you may avoid them before they occur. Whether you are about to be promoted to management and are soon to become responsible for hiring and recruiting, or are already a seasoned manager responsible for a large staff, or a human resource professional looking to improving internal protocols, this guide will better prepare you to talk to executive recruiters in their language thereby helping you to establish a rapport and derive more results.

What you will learn is guaranteed to spare you not only hundreds of thousands of dollars of wasted time interviewing, but save your department, organization, or division millions of dollars in avoided distraction resulting from unnecessary, duplicated searches. You will gain an advantage over your business competitors.

The goal of this guide is to also help all levels of business and career professionals become more savvy, knowledgeable, and sophisticated when it comes to the responsibility of recruiting and hiring, especially when involving a search firm or executive recruiter.

When finished with this book you will have the tools and knowledge necessary to make an informed decision about search firms. You will also know the right questions to ask, and better understand the benefits and shortfalls of the three most common fee arrangement structures — all of which will help you avoid being surprised and realize why you may or may not have received the results you were expecting.

Please note that for the purposes of this book, the terms "search firm," "recruiter," "executive recruiter," "search consultant" and "staffing consultant" are all used interchangeably.

## Chapter One

# ORIGINS OF CLIENT COMPANY/SEARCH FIRM BREAKDOWN

During the nearly twenty years since our recruiting firm was founded, I have often been asked by companies to step up to complete searches that had previously been abandoned. To my surprise many of these vacancies were initially contracted out to costly, internationally acclaimed firms involving significant upfront retainers that were greater than the average salaries of many career professionals. Yet six months or more later, the position remained vacant. I began to ask questions in order to pinpoint "Why?"

Since reputable search firms had been hired in most of the cases, the position should have technically been successfully placed. Occasionally, the reason was due to salespeople or account executives being far more energetic and convincing in generating the contract than the recruiting staff (recruiting fulfillment professionals) were able to satisfy on the back end. This is a problem that can sometimes occur when some firms outgrow their quality control systems and become overly specialized internally. Their abilities can become exaggerated.

When the talent acquisition ability fails to hold up to promises made by account executives, the first instance of a breakdown occurs. This often explains why, after being disappointed by internationally acclaimed retained search firms with offices located in major cities, some companies turn to "boutique" (smaller) specialty firms to fill vacancies. Their thinking — which is often justified — is that there may be more focused attention from a smaller firm than from a large one where individual accounts can get lost in the shuffle.

The next instance of a breakdown occurs when a candidate is referred to the client to arrange a first interview. All too often, after the search firm has invested the time, effort, and funds (depending on the type of arrangement which we will cover later) in identifying and motivating a qualified candidate who precisely fits the client company's job requisition order — the client company manager can unknowingly and unintentionally harm the process by excessive delays with the follow-through. Often this results in the candidate catching a bad case of cold feet.

Yet it is not entirely the client's fault, as we in the search industry often fail to educate and communicate to the client the amount of time, training, and staff expertise that was invested to produce what the client often sees as the final product: resumes that are stand-ins for candidates, sight yet unseen.

If the recruiting industry were more unified, informative, educational, and consultative with its client-partner approach, more appreciation might be exhibited toward each candidate delivered thus ensuring an expeditious processing and follow-through. Maintaining the momentum developed by the search firm is tantamount to maintaining candidate excitement.

While search firms are not to be held blameless, forensic analyses of search firm/client failures have revealed that the failure was usually a result of several lapses — including those committed by the hiring company itself.

You will find the top ten causes of client/search firm failures listed in Chapter 2 which identifies the actual originating source and provides tips on avoiding those obstacles.

Keep in mind there are dozens of reasons any recruiting project or search process may fail, including recruiting projects that fail without ever involving an external recruiting firm as is the case when a company conducts its own search internally without a search consultant's services.

This list compiles the most common factors contributing to recruiting breakdowns that occur *after* a search firm is engaged by a company's hiring authority. Since there is a great deal of money and time (not to mention emotional commitment by all parties) tied up when a company contracts a search firm, being able to avoid failure and ensure a smooth process leading to success can be very valuable.

Three key assumptions made in presenting this list are:

- A written agreement was put in place by both client and search firm representative.

- A search assignment or job description was well defined and established.

- It was determined a realistic talent pool existed for the position outlined (in other words, the job search should have resulted in a hired candidate and was *not* an unrealistic wild goose hunt).

## Chapter Two

# TOP TEN CAUSES OF CLIENT/SEARCH FIRM BREAKDOWN

Search firms may appear to fail to place qualified candidates for a number of reasons. For the purposes of this guide failure is defined as a recruiting effort that was not completed within a realistic time frame.

What's a realistic time frame? That depends. Such parameters differ for different levels of positions within the vertical organizational structure. For example, rank and file positions may on average, require only 30 to 45 days for a typical search — as is the case with a senior corporate accountant or bench chemist. This would be the time period from the job requisition development and search firm contract through offer and acceptance.

For mid-management positions 90 days may be the norm while mission-critical, key upper management executive and "C-Suite" searches can easily necessitate six months or longer.

"Failure" therefore is defined as when the results were not achieved within the appropriate, industry-accepted time frame for the level of search, resulting in a derailment which could have been avoidable. Listed next are the top ten reasons that lead to client/search firm breakdown.

### TOP TEN CAUSES OF CLIENT/SEARCH FIRM BREAKDOWN

1. Fee Attitudes: Is this an expense or investment?

2. Candidate Feedback Delays

3. Weak Links in the Chain

4. The Search-Party Posse Syndrome

5. Over-Centralized Authority in the Wrong Hands

6. Circumventing the Recruiter

7. Too Many Chefs Spoiling the Broth

8. Search Firms That Oversell But Underperform

9. Neglecting to Contact References

10. Uninviting Office Environment

Now we will delve deeper into each of the root causes on our list and see why things unravel and spiral downward when they do.

## 1. FEE ATTITUDES: IS THIS AN EXPENSE OR AN INVESTMENT?

Many client organizations record fees for candidate searches in the debit column of their general ledgers. They view them as nothing more than expenditures with no correlation to returns, dividends, or profits that may have been derived from such an outlay. This early accounting treatment sets the tone for dialogue and expectations later.

Is a recruiting budget simply an expense with nothing to show for it?

When it comes to companies experiencing fee issues, the HR department may not be sharing hiring-success experiences with their peer department managers — whether across town or across state lines — necessary to determine the financial impact that successful recruiting may have had on the bottom line. They may not recognize the millions of dollars in revenue the new hire is bringing to the company during the next 12 or 24 months.

Moreover, these figures don't always appear interconnected in annual reports with any type of parallel made to the revenues, sales, or profits the recruited hire may have provided. They are left for management to consider in a vacuum with no context.

Company executives often revealed that most search firms they contacted came highly recommended by someone else. So far, so good since it makes sense to work with a firm that is highly touted by a colleague.

But this leaves one to wonder why so many of them turn a straight-forward business transaction into a less-than-optimal process through hard-nosed fee negotiations. Minimizing backend costs is often their main objective. Often, when asked about the agreed-upon fee during company visits, most clients were reluctant to reveal the great deal they got.

When interviewing companies who became interested in our services after their previous search firm failed to produce the results they desired, we first turned the discussion to the fee arrangement agreed upon. Only after further probing did it become evident that the low fee they were so proud of negotiating was a leading contributing factor as to why there was no candidate in the office six months later. This is especially true if the terms were *contingency* based.

Everyone loves a deal — especially chief financial officers, corporate counsels, presidents and human resource executives. Whereas line and operational management tends to look at results and what the absence of a manager is costing their department each week. While bargaining for a lower rate may result in a temporary feather in one's cap — the perceived gain may be a prime example of being "penny-wise, pound foolish."

When months later a company is left wondering why candidates are not being referred quickly enough, and a department languishes without its manager, the company hiring authority may have only himself to blame. While a search firm may not necessarily decline a contingency search outright simply due to a lowered fee, the prioritization assigned to the search may diminish — especially when other factors weigh in.

At one point over a decade ago our search firm developed somewhat of a reputation as the "go-to" firm when others had failed to deliver talent. During on-site fact-finding visits, it would often be revealed at some point during discussions that a company official was very proud to have obtained a very low fee on the search. In the meantime the sorely needed controller, IT executive, network administrator, national sales director, CFO, COO, chief counsel, or other mission-critical hire (feel free to pick a title of your choice) remained vacant. Whether the position was a manufacturing or plant operations manager, aerospace engineer, or FDA regulatory director — the consequences of a prolonged search were often staggering.

Given the critical importance of many management-level searches where millions of dollars of revenue (or prevented losses) were at stake during the stalled search, the focus was often misplaced on the recruiting fee itself rather than on the goal of finding the best possible candidate for the position — even though the positions were of such importance that the fee paled by comparison.

Time and time again during scores of onsite client visits and discussions, companies rarely drew the parallel between the renegotiated lowered fee and the lack of a qualified potential candidate to interview.

## SOLUTION

A simple formula to estimate the value of a hire is to multiply the annual salary of the position times 20.

Using this formula, a fifty-thousand-dollar employee may be managing one million dollars in revenue — whether the employee is a sales trainee for a software vendor or retail store manager. Now you have an actual figure (one million dollars) representing what the position is worth. The formula can easily be adjusted.

Of course as we climb the corporate ladder there are positions actually responsible for tens and even hundreds of millions of dollars, such as a department buyer for a national retail chain as yet another example.

By being able to place a quantitative figure on the value of the vacancy you can better gain a sense of your recruiting dollars as an investment in comparison.

## 2. Candidate Feedback Delays

Few things can be more frustrating for a search consultant than procrastination when it comes to candidate feedback. After the client receives a call, e-mail or onsite presentation about a candidate referral, business etiquette dictates a reply should be made within twenty-four to forty-eight hours.

Leaving for a two-week vacation or cruise where there is no cell phone coverage leaves a recruiter sitting on pins and needles awaiting a response while having convinced the candidate the position was of such importance that a search firm was called in.

This is not a beneficial way to develop a long-term relationship. The better search firms are quickly turned off by unresponsiveness, which can be interpreted as a lack of initiative or seriousness on the part of the hiring company, whether it is actually the case or not.

Procrastinating during the critical "hand-off" phase and depriving the recruiter from necessary feedback negates the hard work and effort put forth by external recruiting partners. It derails the momentum gained in what may have been a multi-week candidate search. It also raises the suspicion that the search (or opportunity) is not quite as exciting or viable as the recruiter presented it. Long delays during critical feedback periods create the impression that the hiring manager is not as enthusiastic about filling the vacancy as the recruiter was in describing the opportunity.

For the most part, only average or sub-par candidates will endure a process that proceeds at a glacial pace. The above-average candidates (the type most aggressive company's expect a search consultant to produce) will quickly get turned off by any action that telegraphs a lack of commitment from the hiring company as a whole.

Astute candidates will shift to Plan B and speed up their pursuit of alternate career choices — an action made easier now that their resume is in an updated, polished condition to pursue other opportunities.

A search firm that experiences more than one lost candidate will render the search unserviceable since it risks tarnishing its brand in the eyes of candidates who expect a recruiting firm to represent a valid, bonafide opportunity that the company stands behind. As you continue with this guide you will have the tools to accomplish this and understand what to check first when the process stalls.

## SOLUTION

If a manager's schedule involves a heavy itinerary filled with trips and meetings, providing the recruiter with other means of contact, such as a cell phone or SMS message ability can go far toward breaking bottlenecks and avoiding procedural breakdowns.

Depending on the employee headcount of the hiring company, it may or may not have dedicated recruiters in its personnel department. Some companies do not have a personnel department at all. Should the company find it necessary to have a dedicated recruiter spearheading the interview process, it should make certain that there is some oversight or supervision. Preferably someone who has the authority to act if it becomes necessary.

Notify the search consultant in advance of "black-out" dates or periods of unavailability.

## 3. WEAK LINKS IN THE CHAIN

Initiating a search agreement between the search firm and upper level management and then turning the executive recruiting consultant over to a recently hired, inadequately trained or inexperienced human resource coordinator as the company contact for setting up interviews is a guaranteed recipe for failure.

Clients must have a strong, well-trained, and knowledgeable human resource team member worthy of passing the ball to who can run with it while avoiding a fumble.

During hundreds of cases of failed searches studied whereby the search was important enough for a board director or other executive's involvement it remained remarkable that the carefully selected recruiting firm was later assigned to a poorly trained HR or recruiting coordinator who may have jeopardized the project.

Such executives personally got involved in interviewing the search firms — requiring onsite visits. They would continue to personally oversee the amending, modifying and negotiating of minor points of the recruiting agreement — sign off on the terms, and define the position specifications — only to later instruct the recruiting consultant to work with a subordinate who fails to grasp the process and lacks the experience to manage such a high-stakes gambit.

In rare cases company recruiting staff to whom the responsibility of working with the search firm is delegated had their own hidden agenda — one which was not necessarily congruent with what top management had in mind. In such situations their prime motivation was little more than job preservation — a goal that would be pursued at all costs — even when it came to outside consulting firms, regardless of how much money was at stake for the organization.

In the worst-case scenarios, one motive was to ensure that the search firm failed (or at least appeared to be incompetent), while providing HR time to prove that it could do the job itself if given a chance. In these situations the search firm can find itself in a love-hate battle of wills unbeknownst to management unless a confident executive recruiter sounds the alert. Few do, however.

Our company has had its share of eyebrow raising emails and documents routed to our offices exposing such behavior, ostensibly by departments that were supposed to be working in harmony for the good of the company. This is not to say all will behave in this manner — only that a rare few do if the conditions nurture such.

Recruiting coordinating specialists often are difficult to reach and can make it difficult to interview during lunch, beyond five p.m., or during other non-business hours essential to accommodate higher quality professional candidates who have limited times of availability. For all the reasons stated, it is critical that a well-trained human resource recruiting coordinator is assigned to the task.

If a position is responsible for a valuable segment of the company's business, someone who understands and appreciates the value of time and money should be delegated to coordinate the search process.

## SOLUTION

One easy approach which would alleviate the heavy burden most HR reps are saddled with is to allow management to initiate "exploratory" first-round or "casual" interviews. This way HR only has to get involved for those candidates where managers have expressed predetermined interest. This spares countless unnecessary "first round" interviews by HR and reduces the frequency of pointless and dead-end meetings.

Have the appropriately skilled HR representative (assuming there are more than one choice) assigned to the project.

## 4. THE SEARCH-PARTY POSSE SYNDROME

If you have watched any classic Western-themed movie you may recall the scene where the sheriff rounds up groups of individuals to form a posse (sometimes called a manhunt) to track down the criminal. The posse approach is still in use today in many Southwest counties, including Arizona, where volunteers can sign up with the county sheriff to aid in searching out and reporting criminal activity.

With recruiting, the "Search-Party Posse" syndrome is when a group of recruiting firms — instead of just one — are all put to work on the same project. This strategy exploits the loophole of commission-based contingency search.

What transpires is a classic scenario that has occurred repeatedly during professional contingency-based recruiting assignments world-wide. This pattern is not only familiar to IRES consultants but to colleague search firm presidents who were approached for discussing this subject.

Here's how the recruiting version of the Search-Party Posse Syndrome unfolds:

1. Search firm "A" is hired under a contingency arrangement (payment made upon hire — which will be explained more in Chapter 5).

2. The firm is perceived to not be delivering results quickly enough (pick any of the reasons outlined in this Top 10 list as the actual cause).

3. Company signs another contingency contract with search firm "B." After all, it does not have to compensate to *enter* into a pure contingency agreement.

4. When search firm "B" realizes that search firm "A" has already contacted many of the same candidates and that the problem exists not with candidate availability but with company attitude toward recruiters, search firm "B" places the order on the back burner.

5. The hiring company now has two firms that it views as unproductive. It therefore invites search firms "C" and "D," leading to what becomes the ever-expanding search-party posse!

The root cause of the problem is never addressed however. The outcome is like one bandage being placed over the other while the wound remains infected.

Most likely something must first be repaired with regard to the company's cooperation and interaction with the recruiting firm. Often, a better compensation structure or terms offering a retainer or engaged fee would have been far wiser than starting over again with multiple firms. The root cause was most likely the combination of a problem from our list coupled with a flawed original agreement and terms that allowed the problem to mushroom.

In such a situation the hiring company's practices and attitudes are contributing factors which must be addressed first. Hiring another firm while still engaged with the original recruiter could create animosity among the professional staffing firm community rather than reliable allies and long-term business partners.

The longer any position remains unfulfilled, the increasing potential for negative stigma and buzz develops on the street within the candidate community. This could lead to candidates wondering what is wrong with the position or hiring company.

Any knowledgeable real estate professional will tell you that the longer the house is on the market, the greater the odds are that a potential buyer will believe something must be inherently wrong with the house. Even if there is nothing wrong at all.

Keeping an open mind regarding the recruiting fee compensation structure with the search firm is one very easy, viable, and efficient means of possibly getting candidates back in the pipeline and re-stimulating the relationship. If a recruiting assignment presents a realistic search, one and only one search firm should suffice. But the chosen search firm must be properly compensated for the time and effort required. This is addressed via the correct structure of the initial agreement.

There can only be one winner in a multi-recruiter search party. The rest will have wasted valuable time and resources. Why create bitterness and foes when you are better served by building positive business alliances instead?

## SOLUTION

Understand that a contingency arrangement may not serve your best interests and could be the root cause of the problem. If you seek the best quality recruiting firm, it is unlikely such a firm will be pleased with the concept of working as one member of a search party.

Ask questions such as: "Is there anything we can do to improve candidate flow?"

Or, "Should we be restructuring some aspect of this search in order to get candidates presented more quickly?"

Communicating your desire to reach out to another recruiter will avoid taking the current search consultant by surprise.

## 5. OVER-CENTRALIZED AUTHORITY IN THE WRONG HANDS

Just as passing the ball to the weak link in the team chain can result in a failed search, assigning too much authority to one individual corporate-recruiting representative can backfire too.

The larger Fortune corporations have some form of a centralized hiring process. At the extreme end of sophistication are those with their own executive talent acquisition leaders, complete with a sourcing and recruiting staff that mirrors the type of work executive search firms deliver — while keeping such internally or within a company-owned affiliate organization created for this specific purpose. Others have dedicated recruiters assigned to different business segments or divisions whose job includes internal sourcing while managing external executive recruiters and staffing firms.

When one individual becomes responsible for approving all candidate sources worthy of being referred onward to management, this business model can lead to qualified candidates being excluded from serious consideration prematurely. Moreover, it can lead to individual candidates being rejected for the wrong reasons, such as one search firm being favored over another or other factors rarely considered by company managers.

When a single recruiting gatekeeper is making decisions incongruent with the company's sales and hiring goals, problems resulting from over-centralization and over-delegation to the wrong individual can occur.

Among some of the problems attributed to from over-centralization have included:

- Foot-dragging of resumes sourced from search firms in hopes of finding internally sourced corporate-recruiting-sponsored candi-dates before managers learn of the search firm referral. (Generally under the belief it will benefit job security).

- Extending bias or favoritism toward one search firm at the expense of another (for reasons that may not be benefitting the company as a whole).

- Accepting gifts or other cozy arrangements between the company hiring authority and a favored recruiting firm.

When an individual's ego or job insecurity is allowed to supersede company goals, everyone in the organization looses. A great book on this subject is *Egonomics* by David Marcum and Steven Smith.

## SOLUTION

Turning an entire national division or other significant business segment over to one, single HR gatekeeper is risky. In a perfect world this should simplify things by having a dedicated recruiting representative. While managers may measure results based on candidate quality and quantity, other factors may be going unchecked — potentially for years at a stretch. Executives should ask for:

a) semi-weekly progress reports

b) reports of any *"street commentary"* (what candidates think of the position and/or company), and

c) dialogue and feedback of any protocols that may be hampering the process

The bottom line here is to take advantage of the consultative value of your search consultant, which can extend far beyond knowing where the good talent pools are.

Better yet, require or demand that managers receive a copy of finalist candidates referred to HR, even if for nothing else, it will at a minimum serve as having checks and balances in place.

## 6. CIRCUMVENTING THE RECRUITER

Recruiter circumvention is when either unintentionally or intentionally, the interview process moves through the phases toward an offer without the recruiter's knowledge or involvement. The result is a lose-lose situation for all parties.

Since recruiters may hold responsibility toward the candidates they represent — for reasons varying from smart business, moral, ethical, through legal liability — a small problem can quickly escalate to a serious one and ultimately impact the search firm from a legal or other liability standpoint. This is especially true if an offer is extended haphazardly without a written, detailed statement of conditions or employee manual, and a job applicant were to resign for what turned out to not be the position that he or she was sold on.

Something as innocuous as a surprise call from the hiring company's HR department made to the candidate's cell phone could jeopardize that candidate's current position given the large screens on today's smart phones that prominently display who is making the call.

This unfortunate consequence of modern technology is easily made by naïve corporate recruiting coordinators who never bothered to ask the search consultant beforehand as to the preferred method of reaching the candidate. This faux-pas could jeopardize a candidate's livelihood and job potentially leading to a firing before a new job offer is made. This is but one example of what can occur when circumventing the professional recruiter who can buffer and better approach correspondence issues. (Not to mention they may know of the best times and days for making such contact.)

Managers who exclude the recruiter during key discussions or negotiations also prevent themselves from learning valuable information about the needs and expectations of a particular candidate. Sometimes this information can potentially result in the savings of thousands of dollars in perks that the hirer may have mistakenly assumed were needed. Other times, a serious misunderstanding may cause a candidate to submit a resignation without having obtained all the facts — leaving the search firm potentially liable for lost wages — even though the company's hiring manager may have caused the undesired outcome.

Returning to the real estate industry for another comparison, few of us would think to hire a real estate agent to sell our house, only to start contacting buyers directly after the Realtor© had them tour the home. This would risk undermining the marketing, time, effort and advertising the real estate agent put forth in order to get buyers to view the house. The buyer would also find it odd to be contacted directly from the seller while he or she is dealing with the real estate agent. And the Realtor® would begin to think she has an undermining micromanager as a client.

To prevent a potential loss in commission, real estate agents protect themselves through language in the contract that stipulates that if the buyer sells the home on his own, (should they be successful in doing so) the agent is still entitled to his commission, much the same way retained search agreements are written.

There are always exceptions to when and how a recruiter should participate during first and secondary interviews, however. Such an exception may apply to the conducting of top-level executive searches. Recruiters may sit in on first interviews or facilitate the process to a certain point and then agree to step aside to allow sensitive dialogues to proceed directly. In such executive searches only, the facilitation of direct dialogue can help build rapport between an initially hesitant candidate and the courting client company.

## SOLUTION

Incorporating your search consultant for the consultative value she can bring to the table will continue to benefit the process right through the final offer stages as well.

The search consultant can act as a buffer to help pre-evaluate offers before they are verbally discussed. This provides a valuable "adjustment period" for the company to fine-tune the offer, sparing the awkward process of renegotiating a rejected offer and having to back paddle.

If things go so well that the process seems to move on "autopilot," at least notifying the executive recruiter will go far to provide beneficial feedback.

## 7. Too Many Chefs Spoiling the Broth

Just as too many search firms invoke the law of diminishing returns, the same principle applies to the number of hiring managers involved in the hiring decision.

Group interviews should be limited to only the most critical and necessary team leaders or decision makers in the hiring company. The greater the number of company representatives required to agree to a particular hire, the more likely the chances are of a hung jury; that is, a failure to arrive at a hiring consensus.

The involvement of one or two hiring individuals is fine. At most, three can be reasonably justified (excluding presidential or executive searches involving a board of directors or search committee). When the hiring decision rests upon the shoulders of four or more individuals, all of whom must come to an agreement; the chances of obtaining a group consensus diminish considerably.

Human nature is the fundamental force at work here. If one hiring manager had a bad day or disagreed with a less-than-rave review received the prior month, or is perhaps disgruntled for a myriad of reasons, throwing a wrench into the hiring process could be the manager's way of obtaining satisfaction and retribution. Give someone power and he may not use it as you expected. Whether he or she liked the candidate or not becomes secondary. This happens far more often than executives are usually made aware of.

The result is that offers which should have been extended are sidelined for such reasons. In some instances winning the lottery may present better odds than the assigned group deciding unanimously on a hire.

## Solution

While it is advantageous to invite junior executives and managers-in-grooming to the teams, one individual should have the ultimate approval or veto authority for most professional to mid-level senior professional searches.

Of course, the process differs when boards of directors, search committees and other teams necessitate a group decision during executive searches at publicly traded companies or other large institutions or government agencies.

Limit hiring by consensus to the fewest individuals necessary and you will avoid spoilage of the decision-making process.

## 8. SEARCH FIRMS THAT OVERSELL BUT UNDERPERFORM

As was mentioned back in Chapter 1, many intelligent and well-educated business managers have been seduced by an irresistibly charming account executive representing a firm whose name and prestige may have long outgrown its actual capability. We need look no further than the sovereign countries in Asia and Europe who thought they were investing billions in triple-A rated securities yet saw their money vanish in a few short years during the banking crisis. The results of those transactions were — as stated by one Northern European country's official — brought on by "charming men in Armani suits" that made the sale.

When search firms fail to live up to promises made during the sale, what happens next is the recruiting "bench strength" does not live up to the "starter strength." This is a case of a poor match between the company and the search firm that may be over specialized.

Company hiring managers do have recourse for minimizing this type of problem. It's called checking references, and this does not mean just reading print references supplied but actually calling a few of the individuals and speaking to them.

Business managers and professionals are far more willing to give one version telephonically — knowing that there is no document trail as is the case with email — than would be the case with an electronic or printed document. One can also pick up nuances in the voice and tone that provides another element not available in a printed form letter.

IRES has received written testimonials from some outsourced vendors, which, on the surface, appeared to contain gleaming references. Yet after a consultant picked up the telephone and called the specific reference contact, it turned out to reveal information that was omitted from the written letter. And the missing components were often not favorable.

Just as a hiring firm would ask for references when hiring a candidate, it should conduct due diligence and ask for references of the search firm. Unfortunately, a good portion of the male segment of executives may frown upon this exercise with the same disdain they have for stopping and asking for directions when lost. (A practice which is mercifully all but obsolete with today's modern GPS navigation systems).

## SOLUTION

Ask for placement examples, hiring histories and other documents of information that demonstrate the search firm's capabilities. This will go far to avoid exaggerated sales claims.

Also, try asking for the search firm's *recruiting process,* which should be provided upon request. A process may be replicable across disciplines.

The recruiting process outline should include:

- How the search firm goes about finding and locating talent

- How talent is approached

- Who makes the initial contact or call

- How the prospective candidate will be processed

- Within what time frame can results be expected

As you can see it all boils down to *who, what, when,* and *how.*

You should feel confident and fully trust the firm once you have made your decision, as you will be working as a team.

## 9. NEGLECTING TO CONTACT REFERENCES

Here's a little-known fact: Very few executives actually *call* references — let alone obtain references. At least not when it comes to selecting a professional business consulting service such as a recruiting firm.

Call it an ego thing, but the thought of contacting another president of a company or chief executive officer is, for many, about as palatable as calling tech support and remaining on hold. While companies are quick to check references on behalf of candidates, very few bother to ask for the same for the search firm with which they are about to sign a contract. Yet most search firms will expedite this process by having a reference dossier ready for a client's perusal.

It's in the search firm's interest to provide its clients with references based on its track record in that industry or niche. Some of the most helpful references are those from friendly internal company-colleagues or peers that are not necessarily external competitor employees.

Another reason a company manager may be reluctant to call a reference — especially one working for a competitor company — would be to avoid alerting the contacted competition as to the calling company's business plans and market strategies. When such sensitive concerns are a factor, the search firm can assist by providing printed testimonials, "thank you" letters or citations, or a summary or spreadsheet of recent successful searches.

By obtaining information about a search firm's track record and placement success, hiring firms can eliminate the problem of exaggerated claims (Item #8 on our list) and avoid having signed on to the wrong search firm.

By following through with more than a superficial reference checking process, the hiring company officials can eliminate slick salesmanship that is not upheld by recruiting ability and other problems stemming from shallow reference checking.

If you remain uncomfortable about revealing your playing hand to another company official, you may be able to check with line managers, direct reports and department managers across business units within the current company, as many are probably getting approached by the industry-specific search consultants you are already interested in.

## SOLUTION

It's one thing to obtain spreadsheets of placement success and other supporting documents as outlined in the last example number 8, but it is just as important to at least "spot check" a reference or two by actually making a telephone call.

To avoid any confidentiality concerns, ask for references outside of your industry, and you will at least get a sense of the search firm's approach and style without having to speak to companies within your own industry.

## 10. UNINVITING OFFICE ENVIRONMENT

While large Fortune 1000 corporations don't often have the problem of substandard office aesthetics, smaller companies do. For our purposes we define a small company as one with five-hundred employees or less. A medium-sized company is one with over five-hundred through approximately one-thousand or so employees.

Savvy real estate sales professionals know that proper house staging can lead to important advantages in selling the house — even while neighboring homes remain unsold. If the old mantra "location, location, location" holds true when it comes to real estate investing, then "presentation, presentation, presentation" would be an equally comparable maxim when it comes to staging an interview.

When it comes to attracting a qualified candidate, presentation of the office environment becomes a highly important and deciding factor. An employer is not just offering a job but providing a home away from home where the employee is expected to spend most of his or her working life.

When a candidate is greeted by an overcrowded, disorganized or unkempt office environment it creates a negative first impression. It may be difficult to reverse this negative impact at a later date. First impressions also cut both ways. If a hirer wants an employee to look sharp, then the office space where the employee must spend time should look equally appealing and well organized.

During on-site consultations with clients to help determine why they cannot fill a position despite recruiting for more than a year, office aesthetics was often a culprit. These consultations can be a comparatively inexpensive way for a company to improve its odds of snagging the right candidate before it starts a search.

One such company used as many as three search firms during the course of a year and reached a point of desperation. Once salary and accompanying compensation items were ruled out, the next two reasons for a failure in attracting the candidate of choice usually involved the interview process itself and the often overlooked office environment and aesthetics.

After excluding the procedural causes for lack of results outlined earlier in this list, the poor office condition was the leading suspect in the remaining problem cases. In one company, for example, a staircase had not been painted in perhaps ten years and the carpet was pulling away from the wall. The CFO's office contained an overgrown plant garden that was spilling over shelving like the vegetation in "The Little Shop of Horrors." I could not help but wonder if one of the plants were carnivorous.

Needless to say, this company was having great difficulty getting anyone to accept an offer. In fact it had offers rejected *three times* over a period of one year, despite offering ten percent more than local competitors for the same type of job. Due to the unpleasing work environment, it had to attract at least three times more candidates for each opening.

Oddly enough, the office managers usually did not notice this problem even after raising the issue in a delicate manner.


## SOLUTION

Take a fresh look around the office. What do you see? Do you see areas for improvement? Clutter that can be more efficiently organized? Has painting or décor gone neglected? A low cost solution could be as simple as hiring a painting contractor (you will most likely have to pay a percentage up front!) and the freshened office environment, carpets, and reorganizing could go a long way.

## Chapter Three

# MORE SOLUTIONS FOR SEARCH FIRM SUCCESS

By now it should be apparent that if a company can create a set of conditions so as to avoid the causes of breakdown illustrated, it will subsequently greatly increase the odds of allowing a search firm to deliver the outstanding service expected.

It is not this manual's intent to paint all companies with the same broad brush stroke. We are only focusing on those companies that can benefit from better practices and that have experienced trouble.

Many companies avoid the problems outlined in this chapter, and quite a number of corporations have developed procedures for assuring constant and consistent results from their search partners. To accept your recruiting partner as an integral part of the search process, it is critical that trust be established at the outset of the relationship. But trust must be earned, and it can take time to evolve as the project unfolds.

Following is a list of additional suggestions and tips that can be implemented to improve hiring results:

1. **Confirm verbal discussions in writing**. Search firms may handle a wide array of offers and acceptances during a quarter or semi-annually. And, while individual managers may have a direct hand in hiring a few employees annually, many search consultants process the equivalent of a manager's entire annual hiring load semi-monthly. This requires documentation for everything, and search consultants are best prepared to suggest how to even prepare some documents (excluding legal documents, of course) from offer confirmations to other helpful correspondence.

49

2.  **Resist the temptation to exploit contingency services.** Contingency firms often invest thousands of dollars of their own funds to train and employ highly talented, continuously trained staff who stand ready to tackle your search. They expend more funds to finance the search itself for the duration of the project. The fact that they are working on a contingent basis (paid upon hire) should not be viewed as a free ticket to interviewing candidates just to get the scoop on industry competitors, market trends, or for other ulterior motives beyond the goal of actually hiring. Avoid tire-kicking or window-shopping via the search firm.

3.  **Hiring companies should limit themselves to working with one search firm.** A hiring manager should be served well by one and only one search firm, regardless of the payment/compensation format, or whether it is contingency or non-contingency. The greater the number of search firms that enter the fray, the messier the process becomes while increasing the likelihood of duplicated efforts and clashes between the search firms and the company as well as with each other.

4.  **Pre-discuss offer proposals with the search consultant** *before* **presenting a formal offer.** Rather than risk a tension-laden and time-consuming renegotiation process, pre-discuss the intended offer package with the search consultant beforehand. This is one aspect of the hiring process the executive recruiter can provide valuable guidance with. The recruiting consultant may already know the specific order and value of ingredients that will have to be in place for your candidate to accept. By extending the right offer with all the necessary perks, and allowances on the first formal offer presentation, HR is spared from having to waste days or weeks of retooling the package.

## Chapter Four

# A BRIEF HISTORY OF FEE-BASED RECRUITING

Since one of the goals of this manual is to help company professionals, managers and human resource representatives gain an advantage when communicating with search firms, it is best to have some knowledge of how fee-based recruiting came into being.

First, let us take a brief walk through the history of recruiting to discover where certain methods and practices may have originated. We'll explore where the term *salary* originates from. And since the oldest institutions that employed fee-based recruiting techniques date back to the armies of Greece, Egypt, and Rome, we'll briefly review these origins. Having such a context for how recruiting evolved helps in understanding the modern methodologies and terms we otherwise take for granted.

## ORIGIN OF THE TERM *SALARY*

To possess a strong, powerful army consisting of legions of trained warriors willing to give their lives to Rome required continuous, ongoing, full-time attention to the daily recruiting process to replenish the ranks. This ensured sufficient back up and reinforcements for the next campaign as well as replacements for those unfortunate to have perished. Rome's expertise not only involved recruiting but retention of its enlisted ranks.

It is in this era where the word *salary* originated. It dates back to the Latin term *salarium* which according to Pliny the Elder, a statesman and historian of Rome who described the soldier's "salt wages" or *salt allowance*. In ancient times of pre-refrigeration it was impossible to conserve foods for consumption without salt. Salt was as important to

Romans just as electricity or public utilities are to modern society.

There were guards that protected the *salt roads* used for shipments and regiments assigned to the protection of salt storage warehouses. "Sali" was a valued commodity just as today's oil and petroleum are.

In later times of Rome it was believed soldiers were paid in coin or gold but the main purpose of the payment remained to *purchase salt* and hence the payment amount was attributed to how much salt a soldier's family required each month. It was almost the reverse of the gold standard — a salt standard. *Salaries* were paid so that Rome's soldiers could always purchase or possess sufficient salt for curing meats and preserving food.

## EARLY ORIGINS OF FEE-BASED (COMMISSIONED) RECRUITING

According to a number of historical documents the earliest rewards for recruiting can be traced back to the armies of Greece, Egypt and Rome. One reference mentions *"a reward of 300 sestertii to any soldier who brought another to join the Roman army..."* This was apparently a generous offer since it represented one-third of the soldier's entire annual *salaria,* hence setting quite possibly the earliest known record of what today is commonly known as a one-third retainer fee (most likely paid upon being enlisted but few would dare argue about payment terms with Caesar's sword-bearing generals).

The reward had to be significant since the value in the recruited professional was equally realized as even more significant. In the days before accountants, lawyers, and human resource people meddled in the process, Rome's system was the best in the world and its legions swelled under their various recruiting plans.

There were also other incentives and bonuses paid. Hectares of farming land and vineyards as bonuses to generals, monies left in wills, and more including regular and frequent *outsourcing* involving mercenaries (auxiliary) forces. Because of all these combined methods, techniques and tools the Roman Empire possessed the world's most formidable military force for centuries.

## MODERN EVOLUTION OF RECRUITING FIRMS

During the post-World War II era of the 1950s and 1960s, many companies used search firms only if the search firm required its candidates to pay the fee for introducing a candidate to a position. This was the era of the common *employment agency* model. This was an imperfect system that functioned only for a limited time under specific economic conditions (i.e., thousands of returning soldiers needed jobs and willing to pay for them).

During the 1970s and 1980s the industry divided itself further and split into national franchises, contingency firms, exclusive retained firms (which were growing parallel to the contingency sector), and everything in between.

By the 1980s however, the tide was turning and large-scale national recruiting franchise firms were beginning to sell corporations on the advantages that they would have over the process if they paid the fee instead. Obtaining a higher-priority and more focused dedication of recruiting efforts was one such advantage.

By the 1990s most low-to-mid-level professional or skilled corporate recruiting was being executed via company-paid agreements. Employee-based fees were going by the wayside except in rare circumstances in limited pockets and niches.

This brings us to where we are today.

## Chapter Five

# CONTINGENCY VERSUS RETAINED AGREEMENTS

## FORMS OF ENGAGEMENT DEMYSTIFIED

The main forms of fee structures as they apply to search, staffing, and recruiting firms fall into three categories as follows:

- Retained

- Contingency

- Hybrid, blended or *"Container"*

With a *retained* agreement you are committed to periodic payments and are paying for the *service execution* of what is generally a well-laid-out recruiting plan. These progress payments are required without regard to whether a final candidate is hired or not since this decision is out of the search firm's ability to control. Nor does it matter whether the candidate was sourced internally from within the institution's existing ranks, employee referral, or from another organization. The focus is to deliver a hire-able candidate to that company-client alone as the final goal — regardless of the source.

Generally speaking, the payment for retained services is one-third of the estimated annual salary, broken down into three payments. One-third is paid up front, another third during a mid-point of the project, and the final portion upon a certain date or submission of finalist candidates. This is actually the business model which many professional services work with including lawyers, general contractors, home remodelers, landscape architects, and many others to name but a few.

Compensation for *contingency* recruiting as the word implies, is "contingent" upon a triggering event actually taking place. This event is usually the actual hire (or day of reporting to work on the new job). It could be said that some professional services — such as personal injury attorneys — do work with this payment model. However just as this particular method is used by limited professions outside of the recruiting industry (and even then for specific applications) it tends to work well in equally limited and specific situations when it comes to recruiting. While this may sound advantageous and favorable to the company, that is not always the case, as will be explained.

A *hybrid* or *container* fee agreement is a blend of both. A smaller upfront deposit would be required for the planning, designing and execution of the service itself, while the balance is tied to the hiring event. No mid-process milestones payments are required. The final payment may also be *contingent* on the hire taking place, and if it does not occur for whatever reason, the search firm does not collect this portion but has earned the upfront deposit for the resources already allocated and expended. This creates, in the eyes of many industry professionals, a more equitable and balanced spread of risk/reward for both client company and search firm than a contingency or retained agreement alone.

## RETAINED SEARCH

A fully retained search is often required by boards of directors of publicly traded companies, trustees of universities or colleges, non-profit foundations, endowments, charitable organizations, municipalities and city managers, to cite some common entities that rely on retained searches. Many closely-held as well as privately owned companies in a wide range of industries have used this approach as have the U.S. domestic divisions of foreign-owned corporations. It is the accepted international standard for management recruiting.

Not only is payment of an upfront, nonrefundable fee required, but each of the installments must be paid at some pre-established future milestone. A common scenario is:

1) one-third upfront

2) second third at two or three months out

3) final third at six months, or other agreed upon date

While there are many variations to this, the model follows this basic formula. According to long-time retained search specialist David Knutson, CPC, president of the Knutson Group, "With big retained firms there is no expectation that a hire will be the end result. Plus the cost of expenses and automatic administrative fees are charged monthly and added to the tab". As David explains so clearly, pure retained search can be the costliest approach to recruiting. You may wonder why then, anyone would subject their company to this approach. For many reasons.

In these situations the hiring organizations are actually embarking on engaging far more than merely the search alone; the competitive intelligence and information collected *during the search* becomes as important as the resulting candidate short list of finalists. This information becomes valuable to management and for subsequent reporting to state, or federal oversight agencies. It may also be necessary to help support and explain to shareholders or the general media why one individual was selected over another.

On occasion, payments of six-figure search fees result in no qualified external candidate being hired at all. In these instances, the search firm's *research* however, can be shared with trustees or directors and bolster the reasoning as to why an internal promotion of a college president was a better decision as opposed to filling the position with an outside individual.

The search firm's supporting documentation thus becomes the data that supports the hiring decision if questions of bias or fiduciary duties are posed to the directors or search committee.

With a retained search, a detailed, highly accurate account of every effort undertaken to fill the position is maintained by the search firm, and distilled and prepared in a manner that produces valuable, interpretable data to executives and decision makers.

There are other services performed under a retained search that are frequently omitted from other forms of recruiting such as:

- Air travel to candidate cities for onsite or hotel interviews

- Hotel and overnight stays

- Other transportation and travel costs involving flying of candidates or recruiters

- Support staff overhead for report development and record-keeping

- Junior recruiters working in conjunction with senior recruiters

- Participation in face-to-face meetings and interview sessions

Some of the above services may require additional charges, depending on each agreement.

In summation, the process is painstakingly detailed, thorough, time-consuming and involves a more personalized and attentive approach. It also requires the demands of more seasoned, veteran, search consultants to be able to deal with the comparable level of executives being sought for such positions.

There are many external governing bodies, government agencies, and interested parties that often have a vested interest in a high-profile executive search. Among the agencies that may have such a "need to know" interest are:

- Office of Federal Contract Compliance Programs (OFCCP)

- U.S. Department of Labor

- Affirmative Action Programs

- Securities and Exchange Commission (SEC)

- State Department of Labor, Commerce or Economic Development (or other)

- State Department of Treasury (may fund colleges/universities)

- Internal Revenue Service

- Shareholders, (for publicly traded companies)

- Taxpayers

- News Media

In high-profile recruiting, the stakes are high and the hire itself is as important as *the execution and thoroughness of the process* that leads to the hire, which could be subject to sunlight laws, information disclosures, and other forms of scrutiny.

For example, a Charlotte, North Carolina city manager had to recently hire a transportation manager resulting from a resignation. The manager was authorized to sign checks of up to $100,000. A retainer of $37,000 was paid to a search firm that specialized in recruiting for public transportation managers.

The media and the taxpayers created a buzz when it was disclosed that the search firm hired was the same one that had caused the vacancy by recruiting the previous transportation manager from his former position to fill an opening in San Antonio, Texas.

A vocal group believed that another search firm should have been hired, rather than allowing the enrichment of the search firm that created its own work, so to speak. To this group, it was akin to hiring a bridge painter who was responsible for spraying the graffiti that required the bridge to be painted. Others believed that the search firm that created the vacancy was in the best position to refill it since by having removed the former manager out, has provided some evidence of its knowledge in dealing with city transportation managers.

In another example, a retainer was paid to a search firm for initiating the search for a new university president for a major university in New Jersey. This was a large university that has multiple campuses and thousands of students supported by a faculty of several thousand persons. It also had recently endured a scathing scandal exposed in the newspapers over the course of more than one year. As a result, it had a brand and public relations challenge to overcome during the search.

At the end of an approximately six-month-long search, the university hired as the next university president a person who already sat on its management team. The press scoffed at the expenditure of funds paid to a search firm as having been all for naught. In a statement of rebuttal released to the press, the university justified its use of a recruiting firm by making the following points:

- It felt that it had scoured the entire country for qualified candidates.

- It interviewed the most qualified talent from many geographic areas in the far corners of the United States.

- The process was deemed worthwhile as it reaffirmed the university's presumption that the most qualified individual had been among their board of directors all along.

In the above situation the university search committee now had the findings of a respected search firm which could scarcely find few worthy external candidates — supporting its decision to keep the position internally and promote someone. Having been unable to find anyone better suited (or that was even interested in the position) the search committee felt that the fees it paid were well worth scouring the United States for all available/comparable talent.

It could be argued that without the intense multi-month-long, nationwide search, the university's board of directors would have taken on even more heat and could have been admonished for promoting someone from within without the execution of a search for external, fresh talent.

In these examples the results, details, and data gathered during the search helped support the search committee's decision and protect them from the criticism of cronyism or other charges leveled by the press and public. In these examples, it has been shown that the process can be as important as the end result.

## DATA OWNERSHIP

Ownership of the data findings itself (pool of candidates collected) is also important. These lists and detailed profiles and presentation portfolios are turned over to the client company during retained searches. As you will see shortly, in a contingency search the search firm keeps all such competitive-intelligence for its own profit and benefit.

With a retained search, while the hiring company is committed to the fee on the front-end and it may appear to be incurring set costs without knowing the outcome — the hiring organization could also hire a second (or even third) individual from the candidate pool list and would have no further obligation to make an additional payment to the search firm. It may even choose to retool its operations as a result of the detailed feedback provided.

Ensuring that the client actually fills the position, regardless of where the best-suited candidate comes from, is the search consulting team's utmost goal under an exclusive retainer agreement. The search firm/ executive recruiter is relieved from feeling the pressure of having to promote a middle-of-the-road candidate in order to collect its fee and therefore can focus on the finest consultation free of economic impact should an internal hire turn out to be the best candidate.

The search firm also manages all interviews, vetting, and assessments regardless of whether sourced internally by the hiring organization or derived externally from the open marketplace.

## CONTINGENCY AGREEMENTS

When payment is contingent upon a set outcome, the agreed-upon outcome by definition must occur before the required invoice is sent and the payment is made. For personnel recruiters and search consultants the outcome or *triggering event* is usually defined as the first day the hired talent reports to work. In essence, this is the search firm's industry equivalent of Sears actually delivering your refrigerator. The client can now be invoiced. The only difference being it is doubtful that any national retailer or online consumer product service would deliver anything unless your credit card payment was made in full and approved prior to hauling their top-of-the-line model across the city. Yet this is what has come to be expected of a contingency search recruiting service.

And therein lies one of the many faults with contingency-based recruiting: Would an appliance company deliver its best model refrigerator if it doesn't even know if or how much it will even get paid until it actually delivers? Such a company might send out its floor model or least expensive unit so as to not risk removing its top-of-the-line model off the showroom floor not knowing if the credit card will be approved upon delivery. And what if the wrong specs were given? Or a family member does not consent?

Common examples of contingency-based professional services in parallel industries include:

- Collection Agencies

- Personal Injury Attorneys

- Real Estate Agents

- Certain Financial Advisors/Investment Brokers

- Travel Agents (who only get paid if the recommended trip is booked)

While contingency-based recruiting is the most common form of recruiting, representing the first exposure small-to-medium-sized companies have to the recruiting industry, it is also the most problem-ridden format of the three major forms of engagement.

Contingency, by definition, creates the loosest, commitment-free relationship. It also sets the stage for client-company self-deception, and on a more limited basis, self-inflicted damage (by alienating the search firm which could promote the ideal candidate to a competitor instead).

For example, in the case of our "Weakest Link" problem or delays with feedback, the search firm may opt to take their sourced candidate (which may have required weeks or months to surface and identify) and attempt to recapture the elusive fee from another company — quite possibly a direct competitor — of the original client company. Almost all of the problems in our "Top 10" list stem from the use of contingency-based services.

Because there's no financial commitment upfront on the part of the company/client, the relationship with the search firm is tenuous. In the absence of a financial deposit, or *earnest money* required by the client, the only criterion the search firm has to determine if the company's seriousness justifies the continuing exhaustion of its resources hinges on the communication, follow–up, and other procedural nuances previously outlined.

If the process is not begun on solid footing with a detailed communication of expectations, it can quickly break down for any of the reasons outlined in Chapter 2. Recruiting consultants refer to this as a client *"not having skin in the game."*

When a company makes an initial investment, there is some level of assurance that the buyer is operating in good faith. Reverting to our landscape or home remodeler example mentioned earlier, if the service vendor requires a key or code to access the yard or home security system, he knows the customer will have every reason to reply expeditiously since the customer has made an upfront investment. Most homeowners would not think of stalling the process of returning a contractor's calls while he is stranded in the front yard with a paint crew and cannot access the home's security system — especially if you have made a sizeable deposit for such work to be completed.

Similarly, a search firm could be left holding the bag waiting for a company HR representative to provide access codes to their centralized web-based recruiting portal — delaying the process and straining the relationship if one problem compounds upon another. There is a business *marriage* if you will, when there is an upfront investment/deposit required, which is lacking with the pure contingency approach.

What further aggravates the inherently flawed contingency approach is that many hiring-companies attempt to compensate for such flaws by creating lengthy, corporate-counsel-approved, "standardized contingency agreements." In reality, most of these standardized (and often overly-lengthy and one-sided) corporate-generated agreements create even more problems.

Following is a list of common conditions and requirements imposed by large companies and embedded within standardized, contingency recruiting agreements that further worsen a flawed business arrangement more so. As you will see, some impose such limits on the search firm that the recruiting firm is reduced to little more than a resume-disseminating service with no ability to even consult management (negating the entire purpose and mission of being a search consultant!) or carry out its professional services.

## COMMON COMPANY CONTINGENCY RECRUITING CONDITIONS

- *...The recruiter shall not contact management by any method and shall communicate only with a designated HR representative...*

- *...Only search assignments issued in writing by the company hiring authority shall be considered an authorized search...*

- *Duplication of Submission Clauses*

- *Termination clauses*

- *Survivability clauses*

- *Guarantees/warranties ... to name but a few*

In fact, so many caveats are woven into the average Fortune 1,000 corporate contingency recruiting agreement that search consultants and recruiting firms are almost assured failure before they even begin recruiting! The fact that the company-created and legal-department-endorsed contract must address *duplication of submitted candidates* is itself revealing evidence of the flaws with a contingency recruiting agreement. After all, there should be *no duplication of any submitted candidate* if the search was properly assigned to one and only one executive recruiter to begin with. With retained search, there is no issue with duplicate resume submission and as such this doesn't even require mentioning.

When a company complains, *"That search firm is doing little more than sending resumes that have been barely screened"* — which is a common gripe of contingency recruiting — it has its own contract terms to look to for blame. Since many company-crafted contracts place ownership of candidates submitted based on a day/time stamp (in other words whomever was first to submit is entitled to the fee) — search firms are forced into a mad dash to *submit first* and *interview later.*

Let's look at the first example clause outlined: *"The recruiter shall not contact management by any method and shall communicate only with a designated HR representative."* Nearly every search assignment that has arrived at any of our offices came at the behest of management and only management. Only rarely has an HR representative ever made the initial contact to request recruiting services and then it is usually due to management's elbowing. However, some HR departments would prefer that the search firm never defer to management, this despite the fact that the operational department manager is in the best position to provide the accurate feedback and dialogue necessary to carry out the interview and referral process.

Now let's look at another favorite stipulation: *"Only search assignments issued in writing by the company hiring authority [HR] shall be considered an authorized search..."* Fewer than a small percentage of well-developed HR departments, in the combined experience of professionals questioned for this subject, have ever extended a search assignment. Some required nothing less than cattle-prodding by management in order to communicate company hiring needs to search firms. After all, it is management that has to answer for profits, losses, meeting revenue goals, and so on. And HR is supposed to support and aid management's recruiting initiatives.

Adherence to this clause would guarantee that a search firm would never succeed in doing business with companies that have such a clause in place. It's a built-in Catch 22 clause.

These clauses also preclude the company from modifying its fee — even if someone came along and offered a substantially reduced rate from stipulated "official rate" in return for the consideration of an upfront deposit or engagement fee — in order to create a more balanced arrangement.

The result is one of the biggest problems of contingency recruiting as it pertains to corporations with large, established HR departments. The recruiting contract itself makes executing a professional-grade service all but impossible. The more complex and overreaching the corporate-created agreement, the more a search consultant is boxed into a corner and the less desirable it becomes to work with that account. The results of such one-sided, company-crafted agreements can unintentionally lead to search firms shifting focus to other companies willing to establish more equitable terms while clearing the field so that only sub-par and mediocre search firms remain willing to agree to such conditions.

## SUMMARY OF THE CONTINGENCY ARRANGEMENT

1. The fee is *back-ended*. The client pays the agreed-upon fee (contractually spelled out) upon the hire, which signals the end of the search process and fulfillment of services rendered.

2. There may be little to no bilateral commitment during the search (in other words, there may be no timeline or milestones for producing talent). While the hiring company is protected against paying a fee until a candidate is hired, the search firm is freed to focus on retained, engaged or other projects it may view as having higher priority.

3. The search firm is protected from a protracted, time-consuming search that he or she may deem unprofitable — and walk away at any point since there is no search process outlined or reporting due to the client company.

4. While a hiring manager is theoretically capable of engaging a second or multiple search firms, doing so would be unwise. If the first search firm discovers that it was pitted against an industry competitor, the assignment may be dropped or the agreement terminated — quite possibly simultaneously by both firms.

5. A "rush-to-the-finish-line" approach between search firms becomes the result of a hiring company crediting resumes received in chronological order. When resumes are submitted rapidly at the expense of thorough interviewing this is never in the client company's best interest. Chronological candidate submission should never be placed ahead of interviewing thoroughness.

6. A contingency agreement can be effective for rank-and-file and staff-level professional recruiting. If the need is urgent, specific, mission-critical, or technically sensitive (or confidential) and you do not desire to telegraph your strategic plans to your competition or the entire industry, then contingency is probably not the best approach.

## HYBRID SEARCH

Hybrid search is a blended contractual agreement using aspects of both retained and contingency methods. Just as a hybrid automobile uses two different systems of propulsion, a hybrid recruiting agreement incorporates aspects of both recruiting payment methods.

As with the retained agreement, an upfront (nonrefundable) investment is required to commence recruiting. The only difference is that the investment can be equal to or less than the one-third required under a retained approach, and the balance is only predicated upon a hire and acceptance.

A hybrid search has the following features:

- It requires the upfront payment of an initial deposit/fee

- The deposit triggers the search process

- The balance of the fee is due only upon hire

- The upfront engagement deposit/fee is non-refundable

- Some competitive intelligence or additional services may be included or provided but not to the extent of a retained reporting

- Some travel or face-to-face interviews or web-interviews may be included above and beyond contingency alone

- The process can be expected to be more thorough and detailed than contingency

## THE "CONTAINER SEARCH"

Douglas Beabout, CPC, a certified personnel consultant known throughout the recruiting industry and who has lectured at professional conferences globally, calls this blended-hybrid approach the "container search."

This is a conjoining of the words *contingency* and *retainer.* This "container approach," as the term implies, contains an out-of-pocket cost by the client company up to a pre-determined amount, while allowing the search firm to collect the remainder of the full fee on the back end. The container approach can often provide the ideal balance between the risk and reward for both client and recruiting firm, and it mirrors the approach of many other trades and professions.

Although there is an upfront cost to the client, the net loss potential is also predetermined in the event that a suitable candidate cannot be found or if an unexpected event such as a merger or acquisition or other blindsiding event occurs before a successful search can be concluded.

The search firm also is protected in the same way. For it knows that once it allocates staff recruiters, researchers, and labor hours to a search, at the very minimum, it will receive consideration for initiating the often time-consuming early stages of a search. After all, most of a search firm's time and energy is consumed during the first few weeks of a search project, just as an airplane requires all its energy resources directed toward the engine upon take off. This time is spent analyzing, researching the industry, competitors, locations, and target salaries, in order to develop a rough long list of candidate contacts. Many thousands of dollars of expenditures are incurred by the search firm during the initial stages of each search project.

Once candidates are moving from first to second interviews, the balance becomes more maintenance and servicing, although it still requires great skill — especially during offer negotiations and post-hire follow up.

Companies that expect to get the best performance and value from a search firm will work under a hybrid arrangement. This arrangement accounts for the majority of the successful placements for search firms and has been the underlying reason for many decades-old relationships between companies and recruiting firms.

Under this arrangement the risk is nearly spread evenly, and the investment of time and resources along with risk is more equitably balanced between search firm, vendor, and client-company hiring-manager.

## OTHER DIFFERENCES BETWEEN RETAINED
## AND CONTINGENCY EXPLAINED

Bob Corlett, President of Staffing Advisors in Washington, D.C., has worked on both the contingency and retained sides of the search industry and publishes the blog "The Staffing Advisor." He defines some of the key differences between a retained agreement and a contingency agreement as follows:

> *"In a contingency basis, the search firm takes on the risk and expense of developing relationships with lots of candidates. They [Search Firm] did the work and took the risk; so essentially, they "own" the candidate pool. To ensure they get a return on their candidate research investment, they must present those great candidates to lots of employers. The employer committed nothing, and therefore has no right to the pool of candidates, so the search firm is wise to present the best people to multiple employers."*

To elaborate, since the search firm is funding the search, which often requires an out-of-pocket investment of many thousands if not tens-of-thousands of dollars, it serves the search firm's best interest to position the eventual candidate with the firm that pays the *best fee* and offers the *highest salary* combination.

This might not always turn out to be the original hiring company that signed a contract with the search firm! Subsequently this is how a client company can harm its own interests (as mentioned earlier) by insisting on a contingency search approach. It could be advancing the cause of its competitor unwittingly! If the results of a contingency search are proving unsatisfactory, the client company may have itself to blame by insisting on a contingency arrangement to begin with.

Bob goes on to elaborate:

> *"If you hire a contingent search firm, you are essentially in a race with other employers to see who makes an offer first. This is why some employers feel their interests are better represented by a retained search firm, and some job seekers feel like they are better represented by a*

*contingency search firm. The contingency search firm wants any employer to make a compelling job offer to its candidate, while the retained firm wants the [original] employer to make an offer to any compelling candidate, regardless of source."*

Bob's explanation puts it succinctly. With contingency, you may be helping your own company up to a certain point beyond which the process may backfire.

## MORE REASONS FOR EMPLOYING RETAINED SEARCH FIRMS

There are other good reasons for employing retained firms as the preferred route. Companies that subcontract to the U.S. government are required to adhere to the Office of Federal Contract Compliance Programs (OFCCP) as mentioned under our retained search description.

The OFCCP requires, among many things, that good faith efforts to meet demographic goals are followed in the recruitment of employees. Not only must the company follow these regulations, but any outside vendor or contractor the company hires or outsources to must also follow them. This means that all regulatory guidelines the company must follow must also be followed by a recruiting firm delivering the recruiting services.

A retained search firm, or perhaps a hybrid search firm, is better-suited in providing the documentation that a client may require in meeting these regulatory requirements. One of the common questions posed by mid-level managers who've signed with a firm on a contingency basis is:

*Aren't we already seeing every potential candidate? And if the search firm is having a tough time getting us a candidate under a contingency contract, how is our paying up front going to improve the odds?*

This type of question is often posed by someone who has never considered the dynamics that have been previously illustrated. The reality is that a hiring manager may not ever be made aware of best candidates under a contingency agreement. Not only has he not *been presented with the best* candidate, but the best may have already been *hired by a direct competitor* who offered a higher fee or better-paying position.

*Chapter Six*

# HOW TO CHOOSE A SEARCH FIRM

The reality of today's information and technology-driven business climate is that a search firm is more likely to identify and hone in on a client prospect than a hiring manager is likely to choose a search firm from scratch. Information such as sales figures, projected revenue, plant expansions, new executive announcements, mergers and acquisitions — all of which can correlate to hiring or firings — will spark a call from an executive recruiter to the department head or decision maker. Technology also raises the expectations on behalf of a company in terms of turnaround time anticipated. When a company does find itself having to foster a relationship for the first time, it generally opts to seek out a recruiting firm known to work in that particular industry.

Thousands of search firms in the United States alone operate in specialties that range from actors and musicians (you may have heard the term "talent agent"), to physicians, hospitality workers, cell-phone software engineers, sales, airline pilots, and everything in between. Just think of any viable industry and a specialization or title within that industry, and you will most likely find search firms well entrenched in that particular industry and in constant contact with its movers and shakers.

Recruiting consultants specialize not only in the industry and operational sub-niche (i.e., cell-phone software developers), but the vertical professional title, such as team leaders or project management professionals. Others may specialize only with chief executive or financial officers. And others yet may operate with corporate attorneys and chief counsels of that sector.

Some search firms specialize according to a broad field of work, such as sales professionals while others narrow their focus to salespeople in one specific industry, such as pharmaceutical or electronic publishing.

In many such niche specialties recruiters are so well connected that they often know well in advance when an employee is about to resign, get terminated, or when a company is likely to add to staff to keep investors or customers happy. Mid-level managers and professionals in such industries can almost count on getting a call from a recruiter or search firm specializing in its industry as soon as the firm gets wind of such triggering events.

In some sectors rising-star professionals may get calls from recruiters as often as once each week. This is often to cultivate a relationship well in advance of the employee determining he or she is ready to strike out for a new role — thus being the preferred recruiter when such takes place.

This continuous contact can also present a talent retention risk and is offset by companies that employ a systemic retention policy so as to preclude losing talent prematurely. The subject of the continuous turnover threat recruiters can impose is covered within the book *Impending Crisis: Too Many Jobs, Too Few People* by Roger E. Herman, Thomas G. Olivo, and Joyce L. Gioia. Many fundamentals of the book still hold despite the fact that current economic headwinds have blunted some of the forecasts.

In sum, the mid-level manager or professional's first contact and familiarity with recruiters is when they recruiters come calling earlier in the professional's career while exploring advancement interest. These individuals tend to carry those relationships forward to a day when they actually conduct their own hiring (assuming HR and the legal department give their blessing).

## LEGACY FIRMS AND PREFERRED VENDORS

Another common practice that determines recruiting firm selection is what some refer to as the *Legacy Factor*.

This is when a manager (perhaps recently promoted to such) is directed by a former manager, human resources, or department head as to which search firm to use based on past recruiting experiences. The president or department head may point to an old, fading business card pinned to the office corkboard and say, "This is who we use when you need to find someone to hire fast." Even though the reason for the business card being held onto may have become obsolete many years ago.

The newly minted manager, seeking the least risky route of choosing a search firm is highly likely to take the advice of the former manager, current executive, or HR and approach the recommended recruiting firm that holds a historical legacy with the hiring company. The only problem with using the "tried and true" firm is that it may or may not remain the best choice today. For instance, it may have forgone annual investment in training and not kept abreast of technological advances. It may even be lacking up-to-date knowledge of legal changes that impact the industry and that could spill over to affect the client company.

Calling "Acme Search" because Bob, the former president, used Acme ten years ago may not be advantageous to a client company *today*. In the more disconcerting cases our associates found publicly traded companies with sophisticated HR departments using recruiters that were unlicensed in a state that requires licensing, that possessed no visible internet presence at all, and that may have even been using fictitious "desk names" (a curious phenomenon that dates back to the 1970s and is all but obsolete today).

## PREFERRED VENDORS

In larger companies, the legacy factor leads to the generation of the company's *preferred vendor list*. The conventional thinking of a mid-level manager concerning this list is that, if the company used and added the search firm to its preferred vendor list, it makes sense that a mid-level manager with hiring responsibility would make use of such a preferred vendor list.

One reason why a preferred vendor list may not be as preferential as it appears is offered by Andrew Buck, PMP (Project Management Professional) and president of his own international consulting firm General National, LLC, with offices in New York and the United Kingdom. Says Buck:

*"...For the uninitiated, the standard of personnel recruiting for many organizations has fallen to something resembling the following scenario:*

*The company's Vendor Management System [preferred vendor list] spits out a requirement for a role where a consultant or contract hire might be needed. Since the 'preferred vendor list' contains perhaps 80-100 recruiting firms (making it hard to tell which is 'preferred'), these firms scour the Internet on a harvesting mission ... With this approach, there is absolutely no personalization, very little understanding of the role, and (here comes the punch line) it can be done offshore for pennies on the dollar."*

Buck's background includes global hiring for worldwide major corporations such as Thomson Reuters, Standard and Poor's, and Axa Financial and possesses firsthand experience with preferred vendor lists from inside the corporate ranks as well as from the perspective of an external consultant who travels to companies on several continents.

Chances are good that many of those search firms wound up on such vendor lists by having filled little more than one or two positions but were never proven to consistently fill multiple openings at many different levels. Rarely does anyone in HR or otherwise monitor or grade the continuous results of such firms.

Buck goes on to ask, *"How can you be "preferred" if you are one of hundreds of search firms sent out to perform the same job search simultaneously?"*

Because those search firms are probably aware of the company's "search party posse" strategy, they are reduced to having to further subcontract or offshore the search to minimize the risk of investing dollars on a search that stands less than a 1 in 100 chance of resulting in a fee right out of the gate.

So who are these "preferred vendors"?

They are search firms that are willing to tolerate the near-impossible conditions and terms imposed by the client company's vendor management department. Like a pack of greyhounds chasing an electric rabbit, they race in an attempt to be first back at the line. The better question to ask here is, "Precisely which search firms would recruit for a position knowing another 20 or 30 recruiting firms may be sent on the same rabbit hunt?"

Only when you ask this question do we get a worthy answer: The lousy recruiting firms! Or, those with little else better to do. (Alternately it may be a good recruiting firm, but only the below-average recruiting consultant within that firm will work on such.)

## PREFERRED VENDOR LIST: OXYMORON?

Here's a little secret that further explains how search firms may actually end up on the company's preferred vendor list. Since many recruiting firms proactively pursue a target client company (as mentioned earlier) with what can be an exceptionally talented individual from a specific niche, the recruiting firm already has a professional candidate in mind for a known need, a need uncovered through their network of contacts and daily dialogue.

The recruiting firm then contacts the hiring manager, knowing from industry referrals exactly whom to call. The manager's interest is piqued by this timely presentation of a qualified candidate. The manager or her superior reaches out to vendor relations or HR to have the company placed on its vendor agreement so as to proceed with an interview. The promulgating cause greasing the process here is the exceptionally talented professional candidate that may fit a critical need while the need is high.

With the timing, candidate, and urgency all working in unison to the search firm and company's favor, the recruiting agreement is dispatched, reviewed, signed and authorized, and quickly filed by HR or vendor relations. Presto: The search firm is now on the approved vendor list!

If you did not notice the sleight of hand which just occurred, the search firm is now on the approved vendor list, yet has never conducted an *actual search* for the client company, a "search" being defined as one that meets *full project life-cycle recruiting*. This would include job description development, salary/compensation assessment, market intelligence development, contact and candidate cultivation — to name just a few components of a thorough search conducted in a full lifecycle manner.

In stark contrast, what took place in our example was only the placement of a marketable, pre-possessed candidate — in essence requiring half of the components that go into a full search. Perhaps the candidate was one left over from an earlier pool of candidates — a by-product of previous recruitment effort gone sour whereby the client became nonresponsive (as mentioned earlier). There is no evidence that the search firm is capable of conducting a search from start to finish, however, since placing a previously known candidate is quite different than conducting a full-project lifecycle search.

Should the search firm's candidate get hired, it has consummated the deal and now can invoke the terms and conditions of the agreement earning and collecting its fee. It has earned a spot on the approved vendor list. A search firm that delivers only one candidate in this manner under a precise set of conditions for one specific opening does not translate into its being a reliable long-term partner, however. It means only that it can *occasionally* place talent under the right set of circumstances. In the words of Robin Williams' character in the movie *Mrs. Doubtfire,* what really happened here is a recruiter version of a *"fly by fruiting."*

## SEARCH FIRM CHECKLIST

With all the obstacles and roadblocks outlined in the preceding pages, you are by now probably thinking, "How *do we* go about choosing a search firm"? There are questions you can ask which will help differentiate whether you are dealing with just another average firm, or the best possible outfit available to represent your department or company.

Following are questions that can help identify the quality of the search firm you are considering using:

1. How many years have you been in business (as an entity/organization)?

2. Are you a member of a professional trade association?

3. Do you hold any professional certifications or designations?

4.  Can you provide an itemized list of services provided?

5.  Is an outline of your search process available?

6.  Can you provide industry references or placement history?

7.  Who will be accountable to the client?

8.  Will this be a team or individual approach?

9.  Will the sales or account executive later defer to an assistant?

10. Do you have experience with full-project lifecycle recruiting?

11. Do you actively participate in industry or professional events/conferences? (Being a member alone is only half of it.)

12. Individual search consultant's years of recruiting experience?

13. Does your search firm offer choice in levels of service?

Most reputable recruiting firms will gladly offer a detailed dossier or portfolio mailed to you even if you only asked a handful of the above questions.

The outstanding and exemplary recruiting firms welcome such questions, as they are an indication of a company that cares and is looking to align itself with a firm holding similar tenets and values.

The answers to these questions will also go far to help you determine as to whether a hybrid or retained agreement will serve your interests better. You will know that if you do choose to enter into a contingency agreement it may work in your favor, providing certain expectations are met.

## Chapter Seven

# SUMMARY AND CONCLUSION

Having made it to this point, you should now be armed with a better understanding and clearer framework of the many variables that can impact, blindside and derail a search-firm-assigned recruiting project off its tracks. By pinpointing and identifying the known problems you can avoid them from occurring.

As Chris Forman, the CEO of AIRS, put it, "A great recruiter is worth a thousand times more than an average recruiter." Dr. John Sullivan, professor of management at San Francisco State University who also lectures globally on talent acquisition, recruiting, retention and management stated "I certainly agree with this assessment. For example, in one top firm, I calculated the impact on revenue of a single world-class recruiting professional to be over $20 million. In contrast, a poor recruiter can actually reduce your revenue by hurting your brand and either 'missing' or scaring away top performers".

I can top Dr. John's findings however. One IRES client who used our services from 1988 through 2008 reported just over $300,000,000.00 dollars worth of bottom line revenue derived from 108 sales managers and directors we positioned with them during this 20 year span. That equates to over a billion dollars every few years which gets added to the books year after year to what adds to tens of billions over decades. In this example a single individual regional sales manager was generating $30,000,000.00 per territory and many of such were positioned around the country. Due to a confidentiality clause in our recruiting agreement I can not mention the company other than hint that its growth and success caused it to be acquired and it is now firmly within the Fortune 100 when it was barely among the Fortune 1000 when we started working with them.

We have learned a number of important and specific facts.

**A contingency search can be similar to a boomerang.** Used properly, a boomerang is supposed to hit its targeted prey. If you miss however, it can return back to bruise the user. Like a boomerang, under the right circumstances, conditions, treatment and protocol a contingency based search can be the cost effective approach that also hits its target.

Change any of the delicate balance of necessary conditions however, and it can snap backward to work against you as explained by Andrew Buck and Bob Corlett earlier.

Not only is a contingency based search similar to a pendulum that can swing to and fro, but it is also not conducive nor appropriate to any executive type search that is above lower to mid-level management (titles can vary from company to company). Contingency is the entry-level model of recruiting first time and lower level managers are permitted to authorize.

For any position that is senior, supervisory or managerial in scope — lower to mid-level management — an engaged/exclusive approach is necessary at a minimum.

**For top-level executive roles retained recruiting alone signals the company's seriousness**. It sets the stage to allow for the commitment while creating the conditions and platform that will allow a professional, executive search firm to produce the most thorough results combined with supporting documentation and reporting.

**A search firm can wind up on the company's** *preferred vendor list* **without ever having conducted a full-scale search** (the fly by fruiting method) **and without being that preferred.** This is often the result of VMS (Vendor Management Systems) which as mentioned earlier are actually distributing the same search to ten or more search firms depending on the industry and specialty.

And if you are hopeful to get a favorite recruiting firm onto your organization's preferred vendor list you are now aware of the three recipe ingredients necessary:

1. An urgent hire

2. A sample candidate fitting such an urgent hire presented by recruiting firm (assuming they are willing to provide such prior to having an agreement executed)

3. A cooperative HR or vendor relations department willing to support the department

For those wanting the very best candidate possible and can afford a few weeks extra time without having to force the recruiting firm into rushing or cutting corners, you can see how a container/hybrid agreement tips the balance more closely in your favor while assuring that the best candidates won't be sent to a competitor for comparison offers.

Interestingly enough, when making candidate recruiting calls to establish initial dialogue for top-ranking managerial searches, the very first question an executive-caliber candidate will ask is, "Are you working under a retained agreement?"

Executives know that a company can best demonstrate its seriousness if it has *retained* the search firm. They are less likely as an executive-candidate to express interest, or sacrifice a day or two off for interviewing, if the search is being treated as anything less than a fully-committed retained search. Yet what often happens is when that same executive individual must conduct his or her own hiring, he or she will resort to parsimony and attempt to use a contingency approach.

At IRES our staffing consultants relayed how it was often difficult to convince a company president of the best approach, such as retained or engaged/hybrid. Yet when a search assignment called for the very same president's skills, turning what was previously a client contact into a candidate, the first question the same individual would ask is: "Is this a retained search?"

The fact that this question is routinely posed by top-tier executives, and is even listed as a suggested question to ask by executive candidates in leading publications such as *Kennedy's Directory of Executive Recruiters* (www. kennedyinfo.com), which is often referred to as the "Redbook", suggests the retained nature of the search itself signals how serious and committed the client-hiring company is toward that particular hire.

Arriving at a successful hire is always cause for celebration when company managers, search consultants, human resources and the various internal and external parties all succeed in accomplishing the single goal.

As soon as someone is brought on board however, the next concern a company must address is that of retention. Chances are high that if the talented individual's skills were in such great demand to necessitate the use of a search consultant, other search consultants are already scheduling their monthly calls to make sure the person you just hired remains content weeks and months afterwards. Therefore keeping other recruiters at bay from getting their grip on your ranks of talent becomes the next area of focus.

This is where retention programs come in.

A good retention program is like insurance on a house. While purchasing a house can be a great expenditure requiring a significant investment, the next most important purchase you must immediately make is to start shopping for *insurance* on the house.

A great book that is bursting at the seams with retention programs, suggestions and ideas is *Hitchhiker in the Corner Office* by Orrick G. Nepomuceno, CPC (available on amazon.com). No hiring manager of any size department should be without this great little book on the shelf. Whether you have a five-person or fifty-person department, or are the senior vice president of a 1,000 employee business division — Orrick explains how to avoid hiring hitchhikers (those using your job simply to get to the next step on their career ladder) while simultaneously reducing the need to recruit in the first place. The book offers many low-cost, simple solutions to retaining hard-sought employees for the longest possible tenure.

A good quality compliment of on-boarding and retention programs will go far to reduce and minimize the need for recruiting talent while eliminating turnover and related costs. By keeping the talent, professionals and executives you have already invested heavily in remaining with your company as long as possible, companies can avoid needless re-recruiting and minimize mutineers.

We have only addressed sufficient information to provide a hiring or department manager a head start into the behind-the-scenes nuances and differences between the three main approaches to professional recruiting.

It was not within the scope of this book to address complex vendor management systems or contract/temporary staffing in-depth as that is a subject for another guide. If you have had an "aha" moment then our goal of enlightening hiring managers has been achieved and you may have hopefully learned to analyze recruiting relations through a different prism.

May your company prosper and benefit from the lessons shared in these pages.

*Good luck with your recruiting endeavors and happy hunting.*

# APPENDIX

## RECRUITING ASSOCIATION RESOURCES

Professional recruiting trade associations are continuously evolving, merging, and sprouting off new branches. Therefore, while effort has been made to provide a comprehensive list as of the publishing of this book, this is only a representation of some of the better known trade associations and may not be a complete list by the time you refer to this.

While it is not recommended you go about finding a search firm by first approaching such associations, as many are staffed by just a few professionals and volunteers and it would be too time-consuming for a busy professional to start from this point, one can at least compare a recommended recruiting firm against this list and determine if they are active with any of the professional trade groups listed or similar organizations.

## NATIONAL ASSOCIATIONS

- American Staffing Association
- International Association of Corporate and Professional Recruitment
- National Association of Personnel Services
- National Personnel Associates
- National Insurance Recruiters Association
- The Association of Executive Search Consultants

- The International Executive Search Federation (mainly for Australia and New Zealand)

- Executive Recruiters Association (focuses on the India continent)

## REGIONAL ASSOCIATIONS

- Mid Atlantic Association of Personnel Consultants

- Mid America Association of Personnel and Staffing Services (greater Missouri and surrounding region)

- New England Association of Personnel Services (NEAPS.ORG)

- Inter-City Personnel Associates

## STATE ASSOCIATIONS

- Arizona Staffing Professionals Association (ASPA)

- Arizona Professional Recruiters Association

- Boston Technical Recruiters Network

- California Staffing Professionals

- Chicago Technical Recruiters Network

- Colorado Technical Recruiters Network

- Dallas/Fort Worth Technical Recruiters Network

- Delaware Technical Recruiters Network

- Houston Technical Recruiters Network

- Illinois Staffing Association

- Iowa Association of Staffing Professionals

- Maryland Staffing Association [MSA]

- Michigan Association of Staffing Services

- Minnesota Technical Recruiters Network

- New Jersey Technical Recruiters Network

- New Jersey Staffing Association

- Nevada Staffing Association

- North Carolina Staffing Professionals

- Northwest Recruiter Association

- San Francisco Technical Recruiters Network

- Seattle Area Technical Recruiting Network

- South Carolina Staffing Professionals

- Texas Association of Staffing

- Washington Area Recruiters Network

- Wisconsin Professional Recruiting Resource

- Wisconsin Association of Personnel Services

# WORKS CITED

"The Directory of Executive & Professional Recruiters 2009-2010."
*Kennedy Information*. Web. 05 Oct. 2010.

Herman, Roger E., Thomas G. Olivo, and Joyce L. Gioia. *Impending Crisis*.
Winchester, VA: Oakhill, 2003. Print.

Marcum, David, and Steven Smith. *Egonomics*. London: Simon &
Schuster, 2008. Print.

Nepomuceno, Orrick G. *Hitchhiker in the Corner Office*. Print.

# ABOUT THE AUTHOR

## FRANK G. RISALVATO, CPC

Bringing more than twenty-three years of broadly diverse recruiting experience encompassing several continents, Frank Risalvato has accumulated hundreds of millions of dollars worth of management level hiring expertise.

Coming from blue-collar Italian immigrant upbringing, he put himself through college while working fulltime earning his BS degree while graduating Cum Laude in 1985 from New Jersey City University. He went on to earn his CPC in 1989 and continues to attend at least six educational seminars or conferences each year.

He accepted his first staffing industry offer during November of 1987; and was trained under the mentorship of a CPA/MBA Deloitte audit manager who had gone on to become the vice president of a W.R. Grace division prior to launching the search firm. Within eighteen months he was positioning no less than one six-figure level executive monthly for companies throughout the Northeastern U.S. and was welcomed into the boardrooms of America's most familiar brands.

By 1991 Frank was managing multiple hires monthly and founded his own search firm, IRES, Inc. His ability to fill CFO, COO, CIO and other high-visibility positions for prominent private and public corporations earned the attention of state officials and in 1996 he was the first and only executive recruiter appointed to work with former governor Christine Todd Whitman's administration to help spearhead a New Jersey state government advisory council.

Frank is a prolific writer and has written hundreds of articles for the search and staffing industry, many of which have become front page feature stories. He has spoken at scores of conferences, conventions and seminars throughout the continent and in Europe. He was interviewed on CNBC's Power Lunch program and other cable news programs.

He continues to manager IRES, Inc. and resides just outside Charlotte, North Carolina with his wife and young adult children.

*Notes*